VALERIAN AND LAURELINE

THE LAND WITHOUT STARS

J.-C. MÉZIÈRES AND P. CHRISTIN
COLOUR WORK: E. TRANLÉ

9th CINEBOOK
The 9th Art Publisher

Original title: Valerian 3 – Le pays sans étoile
Original edition: © Dargaud Paris, 1972 by Christin, Mezières & Tran-Lê
First published in *Pilote* magazine in 1970
www.dargaud.com
All rights reserved
English translation: © 2012 Cinebook Ltd
Translator: Jerome Saincantin
Lettering and text layout: Imadjinn
This edition first published in Great Britain in 2012 by
Cinebook Ltd
56 Beech Avenue
Canterbury, Kent
CT4 7TA
www.cinebook.com
Second printing: May 2016
Printed in Spain by EGEDSA
A CIP catalogue record for this book
is available from the British Library
ISBN 978-1-84918-118-1

9th CINEBOOK
The 9th Art Publisher

SOMEWHERE AT THE EDGE OF THE GALAXY... THE SMALL SOLAR SYSTEM OF **UKBAR** MARKS THE LIMIT OF THE EXPLORED UNIVERSE. BEYOND IT IS THE BLACK, OPPRESSIVE EMPTINESS OF SPACE.

ON THE FOUR PLANETS THAT ORBIT THEIR WARM STAR, A FEW HUNDRED TERRAN COLONISTS HAVE JUST BUILT THEIR NEW HOMES. PIONEERS, LOST THOUSANDS OF LIGHT-YEARS AWAY FROM THE HOME WORLD...

... THE LAST PRESENCE STILL CONNECTING THEM TO DISTANT EARTH IS ALMOST GONE. THE OFFICIAL SPACESHIP OF THE SPATIO-TEMPORAL SERVICE, AFTER ACCOMPANYING THEM ON THEIR JOURNEY AND HELPING THEM SETTLE, HAS BEGUN ITS FAREWELL TOUR...

ABOARD IT, TWO YOUNG AGENTS SENT BY **GALAXITY**, CAPITAL OF THE TERRAN EMPIRE: **VALERIAN AND LAURELINE.**

VALERIAN?... WE'RE NEARING UKBAR I. I TRUST YOU KNOW YOUR SPEECH BY HEART?

DON'T WORRY... I'VE BEEN OVER IT A DOZEN TIMES. WE HAVE TO DO THINGS RIGHT... I MEAN, THE POOR GUYS WON'T BE SEEING ANOTHER TERRAN SHIP FOR MANY YEARS...

OH, THEY DON'T SEEM TOO WORRIED BY THAT! THEY'RE WELL EQUIPPED AND SHOULD DO QUITE FINE HERE.

LET'S HOPE SO... GO GET READY WHILE I PREPARE THE APPROACH TO THE SPACEPORT...

WE'RE GLAD TO WELCOME YOU HERE ONE LAST TIME. YOUR HELP WAS INVALUABLE ...

EVERYONE'S WAITING FOR YOUR SPEECH ...

WELL, LET'S GO, THEN. I'M JUST GOING TO IMPROVISE, YOU KNOW...

... AND TO ALL OF YOU, IN THE NAME OF EARTH, IN HOMAGE TO YOUR ENDEAVOUR, AND SEEING IN YOUR COURAGE THE VERY MODEL OF THE VALUES THAT ALONE MUST SHAPE THE PHILOSOPHY OF TERRAN EXPANSION, I WISH YOU GOOD LUCK!

HMM... A BIT POMPOUS, BUT NOT BAD.

YES, I'M FAIRLY HAPPY WITH IT...

THIS WAY—THE BANQUET IS READY!

SUDDENLY, AMIDST THE LIVELY CHATTER OF THE MERRY REVELLERS...

PSST! COME WITH ME! I NEED TO SHOW YOU SOMETHING...

IS SOMETHING WRONG?

OH, NOT AT ALL... QUITE THE OPPOSITE.

I JUST WANTED TO GIVE YOU A TASTE OF THE FIRST ALCOHOL DISTILLED ON UKBAR I. MADE FROM ALGAE!

HMM... A BIT WEIRD, ISN'T IT?

TRY IT! TELL ME WHAT YOU THINK OF IT AFTERWARDS...

A BIT LATER, IN SPACE...

TUMTUM... TEETUM... CHARMING LITTLE AFFAIR! I HOPE THEY'LL BE AS WELCOMING ON UKBAR II. WE'RE ALMOST THERE.

YOU SOUND QUITE HAPPY FOR A FAREWELL MISSION...

GULP

QUITE TASTY, ACTUALLY!!

ANOTHER TASTE BEFORE YOU GO, THEN?

ON UKBAR II, AT THE END OF THE SECOND SPEECH...

... THE VERY MODEL OF THE VALUES THAT ALONE MUST SHAPE THE PHOLI... ER... THE PHILOSOPHY OF TERRAN EXPANSION, I WISH YOU GOOD LUCK!

SHALL WE LEAVE THE WOMEN TO IT? YOU CAN COME TRY THE RESULT OF OUR FIRST EXPERIMENTS!

WHAT KIND OF EXPERIMENTS?...

PHEW... LOVELY! QUITE REMARKABLE!

EN ROUTE TO UKBAR III...

VALERIAN! WHAT ARE YOU DOING?! CAN'T YOU SEE WE'RE GOING TO MISS THE PLANET BY 100,000 MILES?

OH? BAH, NO WORRIES, LITTLE LADY! A QUICK COURSE CORRECTION, AND... ALL GOOD!

AND ON THAT PLANET...

... THE VERY MODEL OF THE LAVUES... ER... VALUES THAT ALONE CAN SHAPE THE SILO... THE LIPHO... THE... ER... ANYWAY, YOU GO, BOYS, WE'LL BE CHEERING FOR YOU ALL THE WAY! YEEHAAA!!!

SO?...

GREAT, PAL! ONE MORE FOR THE ROAD AND THEN I'VE GOTTA GO...

DEPARTURE TIME...

BY SPACE! NOW I UNDERSTAND WHERE YOU KEPT DISAPPEARING TO! YOU'RE DRUNK AS A SKUNK!!

WHADDYA MEAN, DRUNK? I TRIPPED... COULD'VE HAPPENED TO ANYONE!

FINALLY, ABOVE UKBAR IV...

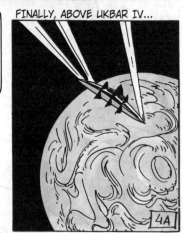

4A

VALERIAN, LET ME FLY THE SHIP! YOU'RE GOING TO MAKE US LOOK LIKE FOOLS!!!

QUIET, WOMAN!!! FOR OUR LAST PLANET, I'M GONNA GIVE THEM THE KIND OF ACROBATIC LANDING THAT'LL MAKE IT INTO THE HISTORY BOOKS!!!

VALERIAN! WE'RE GOING TO HIT!!!

... HIT WHAT?...

CRIIINNGG

HEH HEH HEH!!! THAT WAS A FUN LANDING!

LOOK AROUND YOU, YOU BOOZE HOUND... THERE'S NO ONE HERE!! SOMETHING WEIRD IS GOING ON...

4B

THE BUFFET... ABANDONED !!

YOOHOO!...

SOMEONE... OVER THERE, AT THE OBSERVATORY...

WELL, LET'S GO... I WANNA GIVE MY SPEECH!

WHAT HAPPENED ?!

COME SEE FOR YOURSELF! ...

THERE'S A ROGUE PLANET HURTLING STRAIGHT TOWARDS US FROM DEEP SPACE! OUR ASTRONOMERS JUST LOCATED IT...

THIS MEANS **THE IMMINENT DESTRUCTION OF UKBAR!!!** TAKE A LOOK...

WHEN IT BARGES INTO OUR SYSTEM, WE CAN EXPECT THE MOTHER OF ALL COSMIC PINBALL GAMES...

WHAT TO DO?...

A SPEECH...

OH, YOU!! DON'T YOU UNDERSTAND THAT ALL THESE POOR PEOPLE CAME HERE ONLY TO DIE IN A MASSIVE CATACLYSM?! AND NOW THAT THE CARGO SHIPS HAVE BEEN DISMANTLED, WE CAN'T EVEN EVACUATE THEM!!!

OH, IS THAT ALL?...

WELL... HIC!... EARTH WILL NOT FAIL IN ITS DUTY, GOOD PEOPLE... ER... THE SPATIO-TEMPORAL SERVICE WILL PROTECT YOU! THAT PLANET OUT THERE... ER... WE'RE GONNA MAKE SHORT WORK OF IT...

... LET'S GO!!!

BUT....?!? OH, WHAT THE HECK... WHAT ELSE COULD WE DO, ANYWAY?...

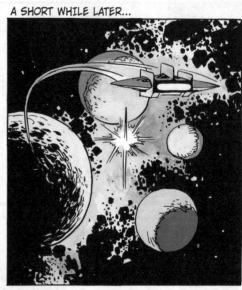

A SHORT WHILE LATER...

FINALLY, OFF UKBAR IV AND AFTER LONG PREPARATORY CALCULATIONS, COMES THE JUMP THROUGH SPACE-TIME...

6A

... THAT TAKES VALERIAN AND LAURELINE'S SPACESHIP ABOVE THE MYSTERIOUS PLANET STILL RACING ALONG ITS BLIND TRAJECTORY.

VALERIAN... VALERIAN, WAKE UP!!!

COME ON, GET UP!... WE'RE ABOUT TO LAND...

6B

8

LAND WHERE?...
OH, RIGHT... THAT
PLANET THAT CAME
OUT OF NOWHERE...
OW!... MY BRAIN'S
LIKE A FLUTMUL
JELLYFISH!...
DON'T WORRY,
I'LL MANAGE...

A LITTLE
LATER...

WHAT ARE WE
DOING HERE?!...
THIS PLACE IS
LIKE A DRUNK'S
NIGHTMARE...

EVERYTHING
LOOKS
DEAD...

WAIT...
THERE'S
LIGHT...

IT'S COMING
FROM DOWN
THERE...

SOMETHING
IS RISING
FROM THE
BOTTOM!

SO THERE IS LIFE
SOMEWHERE!

HMM... THE OUTER
CRUST IS BARREN
FOR LACK OF AN
ATMOSPHERE.
BUT THESE
PHOSPHORESCENT
LAKES WARRANT
LOOKING INTO.

WE'LL TAKE A SKIFF AND DIVE...

SOON, A STRANGE DESCENT BEGINS.

PLUNGING THROUGH INCREASINGLY ABUNDANT FLORA...

... THE SMALL CRAFT APPROACHES A LIGHT THAT GROWS BRIGHTER AND BRIGHTER...

A HOLLOW PLANET!

THERE'S EVEN A MOON ORBITING IT!

ITS MOLTEN CORE ACTS AS ITS OWN SUN!

YES! LET'S TAKE ADVANTAGE OF ITS SHADE TO LAND IN THOSE HILLS OVER THERE...

WE'LL BE ABLE TO GET OUT. THERE'S A PERFECTLY BREATHABLE ATMOSPHERE.

BUT, AS THE SKIFF HOVERS SLOWLY TO FIND A LANDING SPOT...

THERE! SEE THAT?!

HOUSES CARRIED BY ANIMALS!!!

THIS PLANET IS INHABITED!

APPARENTLY THEY'RE NOMADS.

HEY!... ONE OF THE... HOUSES IS FALLING... WE HAVE TO HELP THEM!

YOU'RE RIGHT. BESIDES, THEY'VE SPOTTED US NOW... LET'S TAKE THE CHANCE! IT'S THE BEST WAY TO MAKE FIRST CONTACT!

AND...

... MANOEUVRING DEFTLY, VALERIAN STRUGGLES TO STRAIGHTEN UP THE STRANGE CONSTRUCTION...

... WHILE THE NOMADS, PUSHING AND PULLING, GREET THIS UNEXPECTED HELP WITH MUCH SHOUTING.

FINALLY...

THAT'S IT! THEY'RE OUT OF THE WOODS...

I'M LANDING; WE'RE GETTING OUT... ARE THE SKIFF'S AUTOMATIC TRANSLATORS ON?

YES, AND THEY'VE ALREADY GATHERED ENOUGH LINGUISTIC MATERIAL TO ALLOW US TO COMMUNICATE...

SOON AFTERWARDS, BEFORE THE CROWD OF NOMADS, VALERIAN AND LAURELINE, ARMED ONLY WITH THEIR MINIATURISED TRANSLATORS, OPEN THE DIALOGUE...

WE ARE FRIENDS FROM ANOTHER WORLD...

ANOTHER WORLD? I DO NOT UNDERSTAND. BUT YOU ARE WELCOME AMONG THE LEMM PEOPLE. MY NAME IS MUTAHAR, AND I OFFER MY THANKS. YOU SAVED MANY LIVES TODAY...

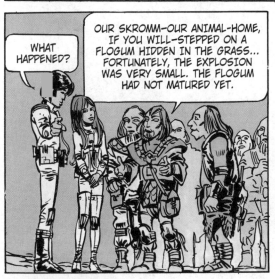

WHAT HAPPENED?

OUR SKROMM—OUR ANIMAL-HOME, IF YOU WILL—STEPPED ON A FLOGUM HIDDEN IN THE GRASS... FORTUNATELY, THE EXPLOSION WAS VERY SMALL. THE FLOGUM HAD NOT MATURED YET.

DO YOU NOT KNOW WHAT A FLOGUM IS? THEN YOU REALLY AREN'T FROM THE WORLD OF ZAHIR... COME SEE!

LOOK. HERE IS A TINY ONE...

STRANGE. LOOKS LIKE A MINERAL POCKET...

AND HOW DID THESE... THINGS COME TO BE HERE?

THEY ARE FOUND ALL ALONG THE GREAT LUNAR CANYON.

I STILL DON'T GET IT...

IT IS SAID THAT THE RAYS OF THE MOON MAKE FLOGUMS GROW. SO, WE TRAVEL WITH OUR MOON. YEAR AFTER YEAR, WE COME BACK TO THE SAME PLACES. AND WHEN THE FLOGUMS ARE READY...

... WE TAKE THEM....

... LIKE THIS.

MUCH CARE IS REQUIRED. ONLY THE LEMM PEOPLE KNOW HOW TO EXTRACT FLOGUMS.

13

MAY I HAVE IT?

IF YOU WISH. IT IS WORTHLESS TO US. BUT, BE CAREFUL ANYWAY...

WHAT'S GOING ON OVER THERE?

WE'VE RESUMED THE EXTRACTION. IT'S A VERY RICH LODE THIS YEAR.

WHERE ARE ALL THESE FLOGUMS TAKEN?

TO OUR SKROMM-SHELTER. FOLLOW ME...

WE KEEP THEM HERE, WELL PROTECTED.

AND THEN...?

WELL, WHAT ELSE? WHEN WE HAVE ENOUGH, WE SELL THEM TO THE POWERFUL CITIES OF VALSENNAR AND MALKA. THAT IS HOW THE LEMM PEOPLE EARN WHAT WE NEED TO FEED AND CLOTHE OURSELVES.

SUDDENLY, WHILE THE SMALL GROUP IS CHATTING AMIABLY...

... A POWERFUL SQUALL BLOWS THROUGH ZAHIR'S PEACEFUL ATMOSPHERE...

APART FROM THE FLOGUMS, THE GREAT CANYON IS BARREN...

SSSSS

WHAT?!

GET DOWN!

SSSSSHH

ANOTHER ACCIDENTAL EXPLOSION?

NO! THIS IS JUST THE WAR...

THE WAR!?

OF COURSE! THE WAR BETWEEN VALSENNAR AND MALKA... WHAT DO YOU THINK THEY DO WITH THE FLOGUMS WE SEND THEM?...

I'M HEADING BACK TO THE SKIFF; WE CAN'T LEAVE IT UNATTENDED...

BAH! DO NOT WORRY. THIS WILL PASS!

ALL RIGHT! BUT BE CAREFUL!!

AND, AMIDST THE WHISTLING GUSTS THAT RIP THE AIR APART...

... AND OCCASIONALLY TEAR OFF WHAT GETS IN THE WAY OF THEIR STRANGE WHIRLWINDS...

YOU DON'T SEEM SURPRISED.

I AM USED TO IT. WAR HAS EXISTED FOR AS LONG AS ZAHIR HAS! BUT THE LEMM PEOPLE ARE PEACEFUL... AND WE ARE NEEDED BY BOTH SIDES... SO, WE ARE IN VERY LITTLE DANGER.

DO YOU HEAR? THE BATTLE WAS FAR AWAY, AND IT IS DRAWING STILL FARTHER AWAY. IT IS OVER.

YOU'RE NEEDED BECAUSE YOU'RE PROVIDING BOTH WARRING CITIES WITH DREADFUL WEAPONS!!!

OF COURSE... PARDON ME.

15

HO, MY FRIENDS! LET US PUT EVERYTHING BACK IN ORDER AND GET BACK TO WORK.

WE MUST COMPLETE OUR SHIPMENTS SO THAT OUR EXPEDITIONS TO VALSENNAR AND MALKA MAY LEAVE AS SOON AS POSSIBLE.

DON'T YOU REALISE THAT YOUR PLANET IS TUMBLING THROUGH SPACE!?! BY BEING ACCESSORIES TO THIS INTERMINABLE WAR, YOU...

PLANET?... SPACE?... I DO NOT UNDERSTAND WHAT YOU SPEAK OF. ANYWAY, THIS WAR IS NOT OF OUR DOING—WE DO NOT EVEN KNOW THE REASON FOR IT... WE SELL FLOGUMS—THAT IS ALL!

14A

WHAT NOW?

BUT, I...

AN EXPLOSION IN THE SKIFF!

YES! YOU SHOULD GO AND SEE WHAT IS HAPPENING OVER THERE...

LAURELINE!!! ARE YOU HURT?!

14B

NO, I'M FINE. BUT LOOK AT THE DAMAGE!

I TRIED TO EXAMINE THE LITTLE FLOGUM AND IT EXPLODED. OR RATHER...

... IT IMPLODED, **SUCKING IN** EVERYTHING AROUND IT. IN DOING SO, IT CAUSED EVERY ONE OF OUR ELECTROMAGNETIC INSTRUMENTS TO BLOW!

I DID HAVE A LOOK AT OUR SENSORS DURING THE BATTLE, THOUGH. ZAHIR'S MAGNETISM WAS COMPLETELY DISRUPTED. THE LEVEL OF ACTIVITY AT THE CENTRAL CORE WAS ABNORMAL. THE PLANET'S AXIS TILTED AND ITS FALL THROUGH SPACE ACCELERATED EVEN MORE...

HMMM... THIS PLANET MUST HAVE LEFT ITS ORIGINAL ORBIT AFTER ONE OF THE COUNTLESS BATTLES THE ZAHIRIANS HAVE BEEN FIGHTING SINCE THE DAWN OF TIME. THE BALANCE OF A HOLLOW WORLD LIKE THIS ONE MUST BE VERY PRECARIOUS.

WE HAVE TO DO SOMETHING!

YES... STOP THE WAR... ONLY THEN WILL WE BE ABLE TO TRY AND MAKE THE ZAHIRIANS, UNAWARE OF THE OUTSIDE WORLD AS THEY ARE, UNDERSTAND THAT THEY'RE HEADING FOR DISASTER.

WE CAN TAKE ADVANTAGE OF THE LEMM EXPEDITIONS TO GO SEE WHAT'S GOING ON. IT'LL BE EASY-OUR FRIEND MUTAHAR WON'T BE SORRY TO SEE US GO...

A BIT LATER...

YES, EVERYTHING IS ALMOST READY FOR DEPARTURE AND YOU MAY GO WITH THE EMISSARIES OF THE LEMM PEOPLE. BUT ON ONE CONDITION...

ONLY MEN MAY GO TO MALKA, AND ONLY WOMEN ARE ALLOWED INTO VALSENNAR. YOU MUST FOLLOW THE RULE.

BUT... WHY SUCH A RULE?

17

I DO NOT KNOW! IT HAS ALWAYS BEEN SO, AND THE LEMM PEOPLE ARE NOT CURIOUS. SO...

ALL RIGHT. WE WERE THINKING OF SPLITTING UP ANYWAY.

IN THE PARTIAL DARKNESS IN WHICH THE WRETCHED LEMM TRIBE IS CONDEMNED TO STAY FOR EVER, ETERNALLY FOLLOWING THE SLOW MOVEMENT OF THE MOON'S SHADOW ALONG THE GREAT CANYON...

... THE LAST PREPARATIONS ARE BEING MADE.

NEAR THE HASTILY-REPAIRED SKIFF...

OK! RADIO, DISCREET OFFENSIVE AND DEFENSIVE WEAPONS FOR EACH OF US... I THINK THAT'LL DO.

I LIKE MISSIONS WHERE WE GET TO WEAR COSTUMES.

YOU MAKE A VERY CONVINCING FLOGUM PEDLAR!! BY THE WAY, I'VE SPOTTED A KIND OF CAVERN ALONG THE CANYON WHERE WE CAN HIDE THE SKIFF.

SOON...

NOW WE CAN GO...

AND...

SAFE TRAVELS!

SOON SEPARATED, VALERIAN AND LAURELINE...

... FIRST TRAVEL ALONG THE BARREN GREAT CANYON.

AFTER MANY HOURS OF RIDING, THEY COME OUT OF THE MOON'S SHADOW AT LAST AND INTO THE HARSH LIGHT OF ZAHIR'S SUN.

WITH ONE LAST GOODBYE, THE TWO EXPEDITIONS GO THEIR SEPARATE WAYS TOWARDS THEIR RESPECTIVE DESTINATIONS...

... LIVING OFF THE LAND, HUNTING AND FISHING FOR FRUGAL MEALS...

AND STOPPING ONLY FOR THE HOLLOW PLANET'S STRANGE RED NIGHT, DURING THE DAILY LULL IN THE OTHERWISE CONSTANT SOLAR ERUPTIONS.

WHEN WILL WE BE THERE?

SOON! THE CITY OF MALKA IS THE CLOSEST TO OUR CURRENT MINING FIELD...

INDEED, AFTER ANOTHER THREE DAYS' RIDE...

SO THIS IS MALKA!

YES. THERE ARE ONLY TWO CITIES IN ALL OF ZAHIR, BUT THEY ARE VERY BEAUTIFUL.

18A

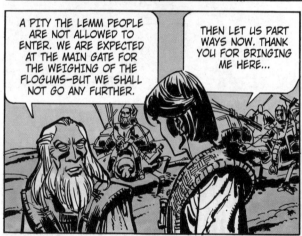

A PITY THE LEMM PEOPLE ARE NOT ALLOWED TO ENTER. WE ARE EXPECTED AT THE MAIN GATE FOR THE WEIGHING OF THE FLOGUMS—BUT WE SHALL NOT GO ANY FURTHER.

THEN LET US PART WAYS NOW. THANK YOU FOR BRINGING ME HERE...

MINGLING WITH THE CROWD THAT SURROUNDS THE LEMM EXPEDITION, VALERIAN TAKES A STROLL ALONG THE WALLS OF MALKA...

STRANGE... I SEE ONLY MEN HERE... AND FOR A CITY THAT LOOKS THIS RICH, THEY SEEM RATHER SCRUFFY...

WHAT'S FOR SURE IS THAT THE CITY'S WELL GUARDED! GETTING INSIDE ISN'T GOING TO BE EASY...

18B

20

MUCH, MUCH LATER...

NOTHING. IT'S THE SAME EVERYWHERE!

UNLESS... THIS SEWAGE COMES FROM INSIDE. AT WORST, I'LL BE PUSHED BACK OUT BY THE CURRENT. I'LL RISK IT!

STRUGGLING HARD AGAINST THE SWIRLING WATERS...

... STRUCK BY ALL MANNER OF REFUSE THEY CARRY...

... VALERIAN IS RUNNING OUT OF AIR AND ABOUT TO BE SWEPT AWAY, WHEN...

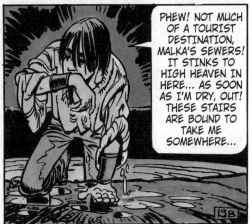

PHEW! NOT MUCH OF A TOURIST DESTINATION, MALKA'S SEWERS! IT STINKS TO HIGH HEAVEN IN HERE... AS SOON AS I'M DRY, OUT! THESE STAIRS ARE BOUND TO TAKE ME SOMEWHERE...

INDEED...

STILL NOTHING BUT MEN. IT DOES MAKE THINGS EASIER FOR ME, BUT I'D LIKE TO UNDERSTAND...

... THEY SEEM TO BE DOING EVERYTHING AROUND HERE!

I WONDER WHAT EXACTLY IS WOMEN'S WORK IN THIS CITY!

?!
UH-OH... I THINK I'M ABOUT TO FIND OUT!

BY SPACE! IF ONLY SOMEONE HAD TOLD ME THEY USED FORCED CONSCRIPTION IN MALKA!

YOU... AND YOU... AND YOU... AND YOU...

IT SERVES MY PURPOSE, ACTUALLY! ONCE IN THE ARMY, I'LL BE AT THE HEART OF THINGS. I ONLY HOPE THESE HARRIDANS FIND ME SUFFICIENTLY PLEASING...

BEING REDUCED TO SUCKING UP. HOW HUMILIATING...

HEY, THIS ONE'S LESS UGLY THAN THE OTHERS! TAKE HIM. THAT'LL BE ENOUGH FOR TODAY.

TWO COLUMNS! NO TALKING! TO THE BARRACKS OF THE THOUSAND FEMININE VIRTUES! FORWARD!!!

AND, WITH A GREAT CRACKING OF WHIPS, THE GROUP MAKES ITS WAY TOWARDS MALKA'S MILITARY DISTRICT...

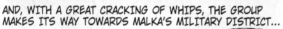

FINALLY...

YOU ARE IN WHAT WILL BE YOUR PERMANENT BILLET. YOUR INSTRUCTION WILL BEGIN NOW...

THROUGHOUT AN EXHAUSTING DAY, VALERIAN AND HIS UNFORTUNATE FELLOWS DISCOVER MALKA'S HORRIBLE ARSENAL. FLAME-THROWING KUCHUKS...

... VENOM-SPITTING TALAMS...

... KLAMIPS AND THEIR KNIFE-LIKE TONGUES...

... DEADLY GRIFF CANNONS...

WITH NO REGARD FOR THE MANY ACCIDENTS...

... THE MERCILESS WARRIOR WOMEN PUNISH THE CLUMSY AND THE UNWILLING.

J.C.MÉZIÈRES 23

AT LAST, THAT NIGHT, OVER A REVOLTING STEW...

BAH... FROM THE MOMENT YOU'RE PICKED UP, YOU'RE AS GOOD AS DEAD ANYWAY. EVERY BATTLE KILLS NINE TENTHS OF THE MEN WHO FIGHT IN IT...

I'M BEAT!

BUT... ER... WHY ARE WE AT WAR WITH VALSENNAR?

HUH?!... WHERE'S HE FROM, THIS ONE? DID YOU BANG YOUR HEAD OR SOMETHING?

DON'T YOU KNOW THAT IN VALSENNAR IT'S THE MEN WHO ARE IN CHARGE? THEY SAY LIFE IS HORRIBLE IN THAT LOUSY CITY OF THEIRS...

YOU BET IT'S HORRIBLE! AND THAT'S WHY WE'RE GONNA FIGHT AGAIN! HERE, AT HOME, WOMEN PROTECT CIVILISATION...

... AND THAT'S HOW IT SHOULD BE. AIN'T THAT RIGHT, EVERYONE?

YEP... I'LL TELL YOU, THOUGH: THE SOONER WE CROAK, THE BETTER...

24A

... 'CAUSE AFTER THE BATTLES, IF YOU SURVIVE, THEY SEND YOU TO THE PALACE OF THE SUPREME FEMININITY FOR A PROCREATION SESSION. I HEAR IT'S WORSE THAN ANYTHING...

STILL... HAVE YOU... I MEAN, HAVE WE, THE MEN OF MALKA, ALWAYS BEEN... ER... TREATED LIKE THIS?

YOU'VE REALLY CRACKED YOUR HEAD! MALES ARE INFERIOR- EVERYONE KNOWS THAT!

WE'RE JUST GOOD ENOUGH TO CARRY FLOGUMS THAT'LL BLOW UP IN OUR FACES, TAKE CARE OF THE KIDS AND CLEAN UP THE CITY. IT'S TRUE...

AREN'T YOU DONE YAPPING LIKE A BUNCH OF VALSENNAR SISSIES IN HERE!? LIGHTS OUT! TRAINING RESUMES TOMORROW, YOU WIMPS!

NOW, NOW, NO NEED TO GET WORKED UP...

YOU WATCH YOUR MOUTH, PRETTY FACE!

WELL, AREN'T I IN A PICKLE! TO THINK IT'S ALWAYS BEEN A WAR OF THE SEXES BETWEEN VALSENNAR AND MALKA! NO WAY I CAN CALL LAURELINE IN THESE CONDITIONS. I GUESS THE BEST THING TO DO FOR NOW IS... SLEEP.

24B

26

MEANWHILE, THE CONVOY OF LEMM WOMEN THAT LAURELINE IS TRAVELLING WITH IS REACHING THE END OF ITS LONG JOURNEY...

HERE IS VALSENNAR! A BEAUTIFUL PLACE WHERE THEY PAY WELL FOR FLOGUMS...

AND, ONCE PAST THE CITY DOORS...

TIME TO SAY GOODBYE...

YES, WE MUST GO A LITTLE FURTHER TO DELIVER OUR FLOGUMS...

THANK YOU FOR YOUR HELP. HAVE A SAFE TRIP BACK—I'M STAYING.

HMM... LOVELY PLACE, VALSENNAR. VALERIAN WOULD LOVE IT... WOMEN SEEM TO BE WORKING HARD HERE.

WANDERING THE SUNNY STREETS OF THE CITY, LAURELINE HAPPENS UPON SOME STRANGE SHOPS...

WHEN...

DID YOU COME FOR THE CONTEST TOO, MY CHILD?

ME? ER...

THEN YOUR LUCK HAS BROUGHT YOU TO THE RIGHT SHOP. FOLLOW OLD NADJIKA IF YOU WANT TO WIN. OUR LORDS AND MASTERS DON'T LIKE YOKELS WHO SMELL OF MANURE! COME...

OH? THAT'S INTERESTING... BESIDES, I'M NO UGLY DUCKLING, AFTER ALL...

LOOK... I WILL PREPARE YOU, AND YOU WILL BE AS BEAUTIFUL AS THIS SAPHANIOL FLOWER I WILL PUT IN YOUR HAIR. UNDRESS NOW FOR THE BATH WITH FRUIT ESSENCES...

HURRY! THE TRIALS WILL BEGIN SOON!

THE TRIALS!? WHOA! I...

IF YOU WIN, YOU WILL GO TO THE PALACE. ONCE THERE, YOU WON'T FORGET OLD NADJIKA, WILL YOU?... I'VE ALWAYS BEEN TOO UGLY TO WIN...

I PROMISE, NADJIKA...

COME NOW, YOU CANNOT START BEING AFRAID NOW: EVERYONE IS WATCHING YOU! EMPEROR ALZAFRAR HIMSELF IS HERE. HURRY ALONG...

AND, BEFORE THE DISTRACTED OR APPRAISING EYES OF THE COURT...

... THE TRIALS BEGIN.

DURING THE ENTIRE WARM VALSENNAR DAY, THE CONTEST GOES ON WITHOUT INTERRUPTION. COOKING, WEAVING, MUSIC...

BURNED!!... NO WONDER. WITH ALL THEIR READY-MADE JUNK AT THE SPATIO-TEMPORAL SERVICE, I'VE LOST MY TOUCH!

OH, DEAR. THIS IS THE FINAL NAIL...

HAVE YOU NOTICED THAT YOUNG WOMAN? SHE'S ABSOLUTELY CHARMING...

INDEED, MY PRINCE... BUT ALLOW ME TO SAY SHE SINGS LIKE A CRACKED GLOMUS!

TSK TSK... ON THE CONTRARY, IT'S VERY ORIGINAL. BRING HER TO ME!

THE EMPEROR HONOURS YOU, YOUNG WOMAN. HE SUMMONS YOU!

?! ARE YOU SURE?!

WELL DONE, YOUNG BEAUTY! I HAVE DECIDED THAT YOU WIN THE CONTEST!

WELL, I'LL BE...!

HEY! THE REST OF YOU! STOP THE TRIALS. AND IF THERE'S ANY WHINING FROM LOSING FEMALES, GIVE EVERY WOMAN HERE A GOOD BEATING! AND MAKE SURE EVERYONE GETS THE SAME.

AS FOR YOU, YOU'RE COMING WITH ME. THERE ARE GOING TO BE GREAT CELEBRATIONS AT THE PALACE. THOSE HORRIBLE VIRAGOS OF MALKA HAVE CHALLENGED US... BUT WE HAVE A FEW DAYS. UNTIL THEN, YOU CAN BASK IN THE BEAUTY OF OUR POETRY JOUSTS.

IS THIS YOUR CASTLE, MY PRINCE?

WHY, YES, PEASANT GIRL. THE PALACE OF RESPLENDENT VIRILITY

WHAT A GORGEOUS PLACE!

TRUE, TRUE. DESIGNED ENTIRELY BY ME, AND DECORATED BY MY DEAREST FRIENDS.

IF ONLY THOSE FAT COWS OF MALKA, SO BLIND TO BEAUTY, DIDN'T DROP FLOGUMS ON IT EVERY CHANCE THEY GET...

THERE'S ALWAYS SOMETHING TO REPAIR... AH, WELL. WE'LL GIVE THEM A GOOD THRASHING AT THE NEXT BATTLE.

AND WHAT'S THIS?

PART OF OUR WAR FLEET! WHAT CHOICE HAVE WE BUT TO DEFEND THE ETERNAL VALUES OF THE MIND AGAINST THE OBSCURANTIST BRUTALITY FROM THE OTHER SIDE OF ZAHIR?

BUT... THE FLEET... THESE WEAPONS... THEY'RE OPERATED BY WOMEN!?

WHERE DID YOU COME FROM, LITTLE BIRD BRAIN? WAR IS VIOLENT... DIRTY... LETHAL, EVEN. GOOD ONLY FOR WOMEN.

WE LIKE THE COLOURFUL SPECTACLE OF A PRETTY BATTLE! BUT YOU CANNOT POSSIBLY IMAGINE THAT WE WOULD STOOP SO LOW AS TO USE THESE DISGUSTING MILITARY OBJECTS OURSELVES, I HOPE! ANYWAY...

... ENOUGH TALK! NOW YOU WILL GO WITH YOUR FELLOWS AND TRY TO LOOK BEAUTIFUL FOR OUR DELICIOUS SOIREE.

LATER...

LAURELINE IN THE HAREM! A NEW EPISODE IN THE GLORIOUS LIFE OF A FEMALE SPATIO-TEMPORAL AGENT!... VALERIAN, MY BOY...

IF ONLY I COULD CALL TO TELL YOU WHAT I THINK OF YOU AND YOUR FELLOW MEN...

OH, WELL... I MIGHT AS WELL WIN THE FAVOUR OF THAT PRETENTIOUS LITTLE EMPEROR!

AND, AS NIGHT COMES, CELEBRATIONS BEGIN IN VALSENNAR WITH MANY LIBATIONS OF FLOWER ALCOHOL, AND CONTINUE UNINTERRUPTED FOR THE FOLLOWING DAYS, TO THE SOUND OF RARE POEMS AND DELICATE MUSIC...

TRAINING IN MALKA CONTINUES, AND AN EXHAUSTED VALERIAN DISCOVERS THE IMPRESSIVE WAR FLEET OF THE FORTIFIED CITY.

FIRST TASKED WITH LOADING THE FLOGUMS ONTO THE FAST FLYERS RESERVED FOR WOMEN-OFFICERS...

... HE'S SOON SENT TO ONE OF THE MASSIVE AERIAL VESSELS PACKED WITH HUNDREDS OF MEN COMMITTED TO THE MOST OBSCURE ROLES OF THE LOOMING BATTLE.

FINALLY, ON THE MORNING OF THE CHOSEN DAY...

LOOK CLOSELY, DOPEY! IF YOU'VE NEVER SEEN OUR QUEEN, SHE'S ABOUT TO PASS US ON THE WAY TO HER SHIP.

IS SHE PRETTY?

GORGEOUS! LOOK... THERE SHE IS WITH HER STAFF OFFICERS.

SOON AFTER, RISING MAJESTICALLY INTO THE AIR, PULLED BY TEAMS OF BEETLES WITH HUMMING WINGS, ALL SHIPS GREAT AND SMALL LEAVE THE POWERFUL CITY OF WOMEN...

LONG LIVE KLOPKA THE EXQUISITE!

WHOOPS! A PLEASURE TO GET KILLED FOR HER, INDEED!

33

... LED BY THE ROYAL VESSEL.

AT THE SAME MOMENT IN VALSENNAR, THE IMPERIAL FLEET IS ALSO TAKING FLIGHT.

ABOARD THE FLAGSHIP, WHICH REMAINS PRUDENTLY WITH THE REARGUARD, THE COURT PREPARES TO ENJOY THE SHOW.

AMIDST THE EXCITED COURTIERS SITTING IN THE SHADE OF A DAIS, A FEW YOUNG WOMEN SERVE REFRESHMENTS...

AND, UNDER ZAHIR'S SCALDING SUN, SKIMMING THE ROCKY SURFACE OF THE BARREN MOON, THE ENEMY FLEETS DRAW INEXORABLY NEARER TO EACH OTHER...

AND SOON THEY CLASH WITH APPALLING VIOLENCE. THE CARNIVOROUS GRENADES OF VALSENNAR COUNTER MALKA'S FLAME-THROWING KUCHUKS...

... AND, WITH GRAPPLING HOOKS QUICKLY BRINGING THE TROOPS TO HAND-TO-HAND COMBAT, CHOKING SNIARKS ANSWER PILIPS CROSSBOWS...

EVERYWHERE IN THE SKIES OF THE HOLLOW PLANET, THE BATTLE RAGES. THE FLOGUM-ARMED FLYERS HAVE GONE INTO ACTION AS WELL...

... AND AROUND THE INCREASINGLY UNSTABLE SUN, CONVULSING WITH MASSIVE TURBULENCE, ZAHIR'S ATMOSPHERE IS TORN BY TERRIFYING ERUPTIONS...

MEANWHILE, ON THE DECK OF THE VESSEL WHERE VALERIAN IS ENGAGED IN A BLOODY MELEE...

A RIDERLESS FLYER! NOW'S THE TIME FOR ME TO MAKE AN IMPRESSION ON KLOPKA THE EXQUISITE!

GOOD! FULL FLOGUM PAYLOAD... THE PILOT DIDN'T HAVE TIME TO USE IT.

THIS CREATURE SEEMS QUITE DOCILE... LET'S GO! THE ZAHIRIANS ARE GOING TO SEE WHAT A REAL PROFESSIONAL PILOT CAN DO.

VALERIAN QUICKLY FLIES INTO ACTION. LEAVING BE THE HEAVY VESSELS OVERLOADED WITH POOR WRETCHES OF BOTH GENDERS FORCED TO KILL EACH OTHER FOR A WAR THAT ISN'T THEIRS...

... HE CHARGES VALSENNAR'S FLYERS.

PUNCHING THROUGH THE ENEMY LINES WITH EASE, HE RUSHES TOWARDS THE EMPEROR'S CITY...

... AND HITS THE DESERTED PALACE WITH AN INCREDIBLY DESTRUCTIVE SALVO OF FLOGUMS...

WHILE, MUCH HIGHER IN THE SKY...

OH?... ONE OF OUR MEN DID THAT! I WANT THAT FANTASTIC FIGHTER BROUGHT TO ME AFTER THIS WONDERFUL BATTLE!

AAH! MY BEAUTIFUL PALACE!! BOOOOOHOOOOO!

DO NOT CRY, MY PRINCE! YOUR TROOPS HAVE BROKEN THROUGH AS WELL. THEY MUST BE BOMBING MALKA AS WE SPEAK.

37

AND...

IF I HAVEN'T BEEN NOTICED WITH THAT, IT'S HOPELESS! ALL I NEED NOW IS ONE LAST FEAT, LIKE...

... GIVING VALSENNAR'S FLAGSHIP A GOOD SCARE!

BUT... BUT... SOMEONE IS ATTACKING US!!!

THAT'S NEVER HAPPENED BEFORE! WHAT SORT OF A NEW WAY TO MAKE WAR IS THIS!?!

HELP!

WHAT'S THIS?!

A CROSSBOW! LEAVE IT!... OH, WHERE CAN WE HIDE?!

36A

S'CHTONK

!

BAH! BUNCH OF PANSIES!... JUST WATCH THIS!

OH, NO! IT'S VALERIAN!!

MY LITTLE LAURELINE!! WHAT A WOMAN SHE IS...

SHOOTING ME DOWN ALL BY HERSELF! MY POOR MOUNT IS DONE FOR... AND SO AM I!

36B

38

MAYBE NOT... THAT SHIP DRIFTING DOWN THERE...

IT'S A SLAUGHTERHOUSE! AND THIS ABNORMAL HEAT! THE SUN'S ACTIVITY IS OFF THE CHARTS. TO THINK THAT WHILE THE ZAHIRIANS BUTCHER EACH OTHER WITH OUR HELP, THEIR PLANET IS STILL HURTLING THROUGH SPACE!

ANYWAY. I SHOULD HAVE MADE MYSELF SUFFICIENTLY HEROIC NOW. BACK TO MALKA. I SEE THAT EVERYONE'S GOING HOME; THE BATTLE MUST BE OVER...

THAT VERY EVENING IN MALKA, WHILE SHOUTS OF VICTORY RISE TO THE WINDOWS OF THE PALACE OF SUPREME FEMININITY...

AND IN VALSENNAR, IN ONE OF THE UNDAMAGED WINGS OF THE PALACE OF RESPLENDENT VIRILITY...

ALONE IN MY PRIVATE CHAMBERS. THAT'S WHAT I CALL A PROMOTION! I CAN CALL LAURELINE...

SO, NOW I AM THE EMPEROR'S FAVOURITE FOR SAVING HIS LIFE!! BUT TO THINK IT ALMOST COST ME VALERIAN... I FEEL SICK! QUICKLY... I NEED TO KNOW IF HE'S OK!

FINALLY, AT THE SAME INSTANT...

VALERIAN!!

LAURELINE!

IT'S WONDERFUL TO HEAR YOUR VOICE! I WAS SO SCARED...

I WAS SCARED TOO... FOR YOU. BUT, LISTEN, WE HAVE TO MAKE THIS QUICK. I HAVE A PRIVATE AUDIENCE WITH THE QUEEN IN A FEW MINUTES...

HA! THAT'S FUNNY! THE EMPEROR IS EXPECTING ME IN AN ISOLATED PAVILION IN THE PARK FOR A LIGHT DINNER...

IS HE?

... WELL, AT LEAST THIS WAY WE CAN ACT AT THE SAME TIME. HERE'S MY PLAN. THE ZAHIRIANS ARE ALL WAR-CRAZY, RESIGNED TO THEIR FATE, OR OBLIVIOUS. THERE'S NO POINT IN TRYING TO CONVINCE THEM OF THE DANGER THEY FACE...

WE MUST STRIKE AT THE HEAD. TONIGHT, WE KIDNAP THE EMPEROR AND THE QUEEN. WITH THE CHAOS AROUND HERE, I WON'T HAVE ANY TROUBLE STEALING SOME SHIP OR OTHER.

WELL, WELL... JUST FOR YOUR INFORMATION, I'VE ALREADY HIDDEN ONE IN THE GARDENS NEAR THE PAVILION!

38A

I HAVE TO SAY, YOU'VE LEARNED A LOT FROM ME... ALL RIGHT, WE'LL MEET AT THE SKIFF AS SOON AS POSSIBLE. I'LL EXPLAIN THE REST LATER. GOOD LUCK, GORGEOUS!

TO YOU TOO. LOVE YOU!

A FEW MINUTES LATER, IN VALSENNAR...

AND HERE COMES OUR BRAVE WARRIORESS! COME, LAURELINE... AND YOU, LEAVE US.

AND IN MALKA...

SO THIS IS OUR HERO! A BIT ON THE SKINNY SIDE. BUT I'M STILL SURPRISED YOU DID SO WELL, FOR A MAN. COME CLOSER SO I MAY EMBRACE YOU!!

38.B

SIT HERE NEXT TO ME! NO ONE WILL COME DISTURB US; LET'S MAKE THE BEST OF IT...

ER... YOU KNOW, I...

... AND TALK. WHERE DID YOU ACQUIRE SUCH PRODIGIOUS KNOWLEDGE OF WAR? USUALLY, ONLY WOMEN KNOW HOW TO FIGHT!

YOU SEE, YOUR MAJESTY, I'M NOT LIKE OTHER MEN. WHEN IT COMES TO WEAPONS, AS A MATTER OF FACT...

39A

... I HAVE A FEW THINGS HERE THAT YOU MIGHT FIND INTERESTING. LIKE THIS, FOR EXAMPLE...

WHAT IS IT?

A LIGHT STUNNER.

A STUNNER?
HOW DOES IT WORK?

... LIKE THIS. SORRY, MY GOOD WOMAN...

... BUT FOR THE QUEEN OF THE AMAZONS I FIND YOU RATHER CARELESS. NOW I'VE GOT TO CARRY THIS DEAD WEIGHT TO A SHIP. NOT AN EASY JOB...

PHEW... NOT AN EASY JOB AT ALL... I'M LUCKY, THOUGH. THIS PART OF THE PALACE SEEMS DESERTED.

39B

THE ROYAL FLAGSHIP! IF ONLY... **RATS!** GUARDS! QUICK, MY STUNNER!

WHO GOES THERE?

AND...

OK, ALL ABOARD! THERE'S NOT A MINUTE TO LOSE NOW; I DON'T WANT EVERY VIRAGO IN MALKA AFTER ME!

HEADING TO THE SKIFF. I'LL CALL LAURELINE ON THE WAY...

AT THAT MOMENT IN VALSENNAR...

THERE, DONE! ONE SLEEPING PILL IN THAT ARISTOCRATIC ALCOHOLIC'S CUP...

... AND I CAN GO. I'LL CALL VALERIAN AND TELL HIM I DID IT.

IN THE TROUBLED, STUFFY NIGHT OF ZAHIR, LAURELINE'S FLYER IS SOON ON ITS WAY TO THE CANYON, LIKE THAT OF VALERIAN, WHO HAS JUST RADIOED HER...

LAURELINE? IT WORKED FOR ME, I'M HEADING FOR THE SKIFF. WHAT'S YOUR STATUS?

MISSION ACCOMPLISHED. I'M ON MY WAY TOO!

A FEW HOURS LATER...

SO. THE SKIFF IS READY. KLOPKA'S STARTING TO STIR... AND HERE COMES LAURELINE!

MAY I INTRODUCE EMPEROR ALZAFRAR? HE'S STILL A BIT SLEEPY, BUT HE'LL BE ALL RIGHT.

AND THIS IS QUEEN KLOPKA. SLIGHTLY GROGGY BUT ALREADY AWAKE... COME THIS WAY NOW SO I CAN EXPLAIN...

THE SITUATION IS DIRE! WHILE I WAS WAITING FOR YOU, I TOOK A FEW SENSOR READINGS. YESTERDAY'S BATTLE HAS THROWN ZAHIR OFF COURSE FOR GOOD. IT'S NOW WITHIN THE GRAVITATIONAL WELL OF UKBAR'S STAR. WE ONLY HAVE A FEW DAYS TO ACT...

WHAT DO YOU INTEND TO DO?

WE'RE GOING TO NEED THE ZAHIRIANS' COLLABORATION. BUT FIRST, THEY HAVE TO UNDERSTAND WHAT THE UNIVERSE IS! SO, FIRST OF ALL, WE TAKE THEM TO SEE THE STARS. THEN...

WHAT...

PAK

OW

WHOA! WHOA! NOW'S NOT THE TIME!!

IT'S THAT SHREW! SHE ATTACKED ME WITHOUT WARNING!!!

THIS JACKANAPES SPLASHES HIMSELF WITH FLOWER ALCOHOL... TO WAKE HIMSELF UP, HE SAYS!! BLARGH! THE STINK...

I DON'T UNDERSTAND! WHERE ARE WE? WHAT ARE ALL THOSE LITTLE LIGHTS DOING UP THERE?

PFFF! YOU IDIOT... CAN'T YOU SEE THESE ARE PFITZ STONES SEWN ONTO AN ENORMOUS BLANKET OF BLACK FUFUNIL FABRIC! IT'S OBVIOUS, REALLY.

ERM... I DON'T MEAN TO CONTRADICT YOU, YOUR MAJESTY, BUT THAT'S NOT EXACTLY IT. AROUND US IS THE VOID. AND EACH OF THOSE LITTLE LIGHTS IS A SUN, NEXT TO WHICH ARE OTHER WORLDS LIKE ZAHIR...

THE V... V... VOID?!

OTHER ZAHIRS!? IMPOSSSSSS...

WHAT HAPPENED?

THE POOR DEARS PASSED OUT!

BOOM 33

43A

LATER, IN THE LARGE TERRAN SHIP'S HYPNO-LIBRARY, AFTER A LONG SESSION OF FORCED MEMORISATION UNDER HYPNOSIS...

YOU HAVE TO ADMIT, IT MUST BE QUITE A SHOCK FOR THE INHABITANTS OF A CLOSED WORLD TO DISCOVER THE STARS... WE'RE GOING TO HAVE TO GIVE THEM INTENSIVE HYPNO-EDUCATION.

GOT IT. HEADING FOR THE SHIP!

SO THAT'S WHAT THE UNIVERSE IS! OH, MY HEAD HURTS...

WIMP! I UNDERSTOOD EVERYTHING EASILY!

OK. LISTEN TO ME, BOTH OF YOU... YOU NOW KNOW THAT ZAHIR IS DOOMED IF WE DON'T ACT IMMEDIATELY! I THINK I'VE FOUND A WAY TO STOP YOUR WORLD'S HEADLONG PLUNGE. TO DO THAT...

43B

... I NEED YOUR WHOLE STOCK OF FLOGUMS. EVERY SINGLE ONE, YOU HEAR?!! THE LEMM PEOPLE, WHO ARE SKILLED IN THEIR HANDLING, WILL HAVE TO ASSIST YOU, AND MY FRIEND LAURELINE WILL BRING THEM HERE. CAN I COUNT ON YOUR HELP?...

YOU CAN, EARTHLING!

PERFECT, THEN! YOU'RE GOING TO GO BACK TO YOUR RESPECTIVE CITIES. THE SLIGHTEST DELAY WOULD DOOM US ALL AND WOULD ALSO MEAN DEATH FOR ALL THE COLONISTS OF UKBAR WHOSE EXISTENCE YOU JUST DISCOVERED...

44A

A SCANT FEW HOURS HAVE PASSED WHEN A DESPERATE ACTIVITY FILLS ZAHIR OF THE BURNING SUN, THE STRANGE LAND WITHOUT STARS...

EVERYWHERE, AS IF BY A MIRACLE, THE LOOMING DANGER ERASES THE WEIGHT OF THE UNMOVING PAST. IN MALKA, IN VALSENNAR AND AMONG THE LEMM PEOPLE...

... THE ZAHIRIANS, UNITED FOR THE FIRST TIME, MEN AND WOMEN WORKING SIDE BY SIDE, STRUGGLE TO SAVE THEIR PLANET IN DISTRESS.

44B

AND, WHILE VALERIAN IS LOST IN COMPLEX CALCULATIONS...

... LAURELINE TRANSPORTS FLOGUMS TO THE SHIP BY THE HUNDREDS...

FINALLY...

IT'S DONE, VALERIAN. EVERY FLOGUM WE COULD LAY OUR HANDS ON HAS BEEN BROUGHT TO THE MAGAZINE, AND THEIR AUTOMATIC DEPLOYMENT HAS BEEN PROGRAMMED ACCORDING TO YOUR NUMBERS.

I'M DONE HERE AS WELL.

45A

WILL YOU FINALLY TELL ME WHAT YOU HAVE IN MIND?

YES. I'M GOING TO FIGHT FIRE WITH FIRE BY DROPPING FLOGUMS IN A CONCENTRIC PATTERN AROUND ZAHIR AND JUMPING THROUGH SPACE-TIME SO THEY EXPLODE SIMULTANEOUSLY! THAT WAY I SHOULD BE ABLE TO BREAK THE MOMENTUM OF THE PLANET AND SET IT ON A STABLE ORBIT AROUND UKBAR.

BUT... ZAHIR WILL BE TORN TO PIECES!

I DON'T THINK SO. I'VE WORKED IT ALL OUT: THE RISK OF EXPLOSION IN THE CORE, THE POSSIBILITY OF THE CRUST CRACKING ALONG THE GREAT CANYON, AND PLENTY MORE THINGS. IT SHOULD HOLD! THERE! THE JUMP IS SCHEDULED FOR THREE HOURS FROM NOW. YOU HAVE JUST ENOUGH TIME TO WARN OUR ZAHIRIAN FRIENDS.

A TIME OF UNBEARABLE FEAR BEGINS INSIDE ZAHIR...

READY, LAURELINE? **NOW!**

... AS WELL AS ON THE PLANETS OF UKBAR, IN CONSTANT VIDEO CONTACT WITH THE SHIP. SUDDENLY...

45B

47

... WITH A PRODIGIOUS WHITE FLASH, THE ENTIRE PLANET SEEMS TO STRETCH AND TWIST, LIKE DOUGH WHIPPED BY THE STRING OF EXPLOSIVES VALERIAN HAS WOVEN AROUND IT.

MUCH LATER...

IT'S FANTASTIC! YOU DID IT, VALERIAN! THE UKBAR SYSTEM NOW COUNTS FIVE PLANETS IN PERFECT WORKING ORDER!!

YEP... ON TOP OF THAT, THE FIRST CONTACTS BETWEEN COLONISTS AND ZAHIRIANS ARE EXCELLENT.

YOU KNOW WHAT ELSE I HEARD? ZAHIR'S WHOLE SOCIETY IS COLLAPSING. THERE'S A VERITABLE EPIDEMIC OF MARRIAGES! THEY EVEN SAY THAT QUEEN KLOPKA HAS DECIDED TO MARRY EMPEROR ALZAFRAR!!! THE POOR MAN IS GOING TO DROWN IN FLOWER ALCOHOL FOR GOOD...

SPEAKING OF WHICH... WHAT ARE YOU DOING? THIS SMELL...

ME?... HIC... NOTHING! I'VE FINALLY FOUND THE TIME TO... SAMPLE ZAHIRIAN PRODUCTS... ANYWAY, I'VE BEEN THINKING... I'VE GOT NOTHING AGAINST MATRIARCHY... SEE? I'M LETTING YOU BRING US BACK TO GALAXITY!... AND BE QUICK ABOUT IT!

P. CHRISTIN
J.C. MEZIERES

THE END

48